Left Hand Writing

Most handwriting resources for schools and parents work well – for right-handers. Unfortunately, the needs of left-handed children are often overlooked. For example, illustrations or letters that should be copied by the child are often obscured by the left-hander as soon as the hand reaches the paper!

The un-trained left-handed writer also often encounters the problem of 'smudging' as the left hand drags over work which has just been written. This can lead to a great deal of frustration and loss of self-esteem, and result in difficulties not just in handwriting but in other literacy skills.

This book – **Left Hand Writing Skills** – now provides a specially-designed learning programme which is ideal for parents and teachers of left-handers. The programme is available for home use in a series of three separate and colourful titles. Each covers one of the three essential stages for the establishment of good handwriting habits:

1. **fine motor control**
2. **letter formation and flow**
3. **successful smudge-free writing**

In this combined edition, the three stages are presented in one volume, with mono worksheets which can be photocopied for use in schools.

The Stage 1 worksheets provide extensive opportunities for the child to practise the preliminaries for handwriting. These include correct grip, appropriate and comfortable positioning of the paper, and the detailed movement and hand-eye co-ordination needed to produce accurately the straight and curved elements of the letters of the alphabet. Stage 2 focuses on letter joins and word formation. Stage 3 provides more educational worksheets which should consolidate good left hand writing habits.

All the books in this series have been laid out to support the left-handed writer. They are all spiral bound at the top of the page. For the home edition, this ensures that the writer always meets a flat A4 worksheet that can be positioned correctly for left hand use, and it avoids there being any obstacle from the left hand side. In this book, top binding ensures that the binding itself does not interfere with the contents of the worksheet once it has been photocopied.

Initially, with this binding, every other worksheet will appear to be upside-down! Once they are in use, however, they are obviously the right way up, and their benefits will soon be found!

The following icons will be used as reminders throughout the book:

Paper Position

The use of this icon reminds the student how to position the paper at an angle.

Pencil or Pen hold

The use of this icon reminds the student how to hold the pencil or pen correctly, and evolves through the three stages of the programme.

Introduction

Handwriting is an important skill. Acquiring it takes perseverance and practice, whether the writer is left-handed or right-handed. For the left-handed, though, development of the skill of handwriting – in the 'right-handed' world where text runs from left to right – needs just a little more help.

Despite any initial difficulties, with good, regular practice and patient guidance from adults, left-handers can write just as well – and often better – than their right-handed friends. Five to ten minutes of regular daily practice is needed – and this is far more effective than occasional lengthy sessions.

The exercises in this book are intended to be used by the child under adult guidance. The adult needs to read the instructions to – or with – the student and make sure that the student understands how to form the letters and joins correctly. For fluent, neat, legible handwriting to develop, it is important for the child from the start to establish accurate letter formation, smooth and consistent joins and even letter sizing.

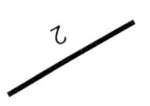

The student and adult team should, therefore, work through the book, practising each skill carefully before moving on to the next. The

According to the National Handwriting Association, the series is "... a structured and attractive course that could help a left-hander to become a competent, confident writer." – and which, according to the Head of School Improvement and Achievement, Worcester LEA "... will help to improve the writing skills of all left-handers: a valuable resource for teachers and parents."

handwriting style in this book has been chosen to help the student write evenly and fluently. However, each child will eventually develop his or her own unique style.

Where necessary, other activities can be added, such as those suggested in the 'Top Tips' and 'Check this out' sections in the worksheets of the first two Stages.

Top Tip: *Watch out for these important reminders.*

Check this out!

Watch out for these important reminders.

2

Basics for successful skill Development

Sit Comfortably

Make sure that the left-hander is sitting in a comfortable position and that the desk or table they are using is not too high. Use a cushion on the seat if necessary. Also, ensure that left-handers have plenty of elbow room so that, if they are working close to others, they won't clash elbows with right-handed neighbours.

Paper Position

It can be helpful for the left-handed student to turn their paper at an angle. This allows the arm to move freely in line with the hand across the page. Turn the top of the page until the arrow is pointing away from the student and the base of the icon lines up with the edge of the writing table or desk. This will help develop a consistent working position.

Pencil or Pen Hold

It is generally acknowledged that the best way to hold a pencil or pen is in the 'tripod' grip, that is, using three fingers. The pencil rests on the middle finger and is gripped either side by the thumb and forefinger. The pencil should be held about 1.5 cm away from the tip to allow the writing to be seen more clearly. It also keeps the fingers away from the writing.

Recommended pencil hold and paper position.

This minimises the likelihood of smudging when using ink pens, and it ensures that the fingers are kept above the nib. Gripping a pencil too tightly is a common problem. It will not improve the handwriting and causes the hand to tire quickly. Use of chunky pencils and grips is helpful.

Word Spacing

Correct spacing between words can be a problem for left-handers. It is quite usual for teachers to tell all their pupils to "... leave a finger space between words". The student is encouraged to put their finger (a left-handed finger is assumed!) at the end of a word and to begin writing the next word immediately after their finger. This works well for the right-hander but it leaves left-handers doing contortions! Instead, teachers should encourage the left-hander to leave the space required for a letter 'O' between their words.

Contents

Stage 1	Worksheets 1-28	6-33
	Stage 1 Alphabet Reference Sheet	34
	Stage 1 Number Reference Sheet	35
Stage 2	Worksheets 1-28	37-64
	Stages 2 and 3 Alphabet Reference Sheet (lower case)	65
	Stages 2 and 3 Alphabet Reference Sheet (capitals)	66
Stage 3	Worksheets 1-27	68-94
	Stages 2 and 3 Number Reference Sheet	95
	Practice Sheet	96
	More help for left-handers	97
	Contacts	98

4

Stage 1

fabulous fine motor practice

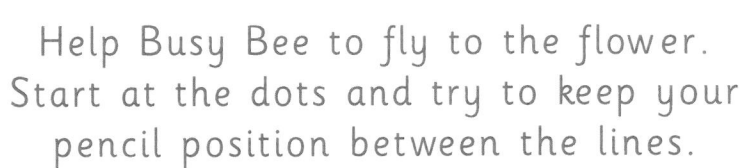

Remember to hold your pencil correctly.

STAGE 1   WORKSHEET   1

Help Busy Bee to fly to the flower.
Start at the dots and try to keep your
pencil position between the lines.

Top Tip: Make sure the child always begins on the left.

Remember to line up the base of this icon with the edge of your table.

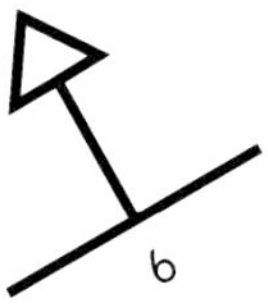

Remember to hold your pencil correctly.

STAGE 1   WORKSHEET   2

Follow Sally Snail's trail. Start at the dots.

Top Tip: *If the child finds it difficult to keep within the lines then try other activities to increase co-ordination. Playing with Playdough helps to develop strength in the fingers. Lacing beads and sewing cards help to develop co-ordination.*

Remember to line up the base of this icon with the edge of your table.

Remember to hold your pencil correctly.

STAGE 1 WORKSHEET 3

Help Willie Woodlouse find his way home.

Top Tip: Mazes are a fun way to improve pencil control. Try drawing some mazes for the child to use.

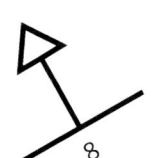

Remember to line up the base of this icon with the edge of your table.

Remember to hold your pencil correctly.

STAGE 1 WORKSHEET 4

Hop after Grasshopper Green. Start at the dots.

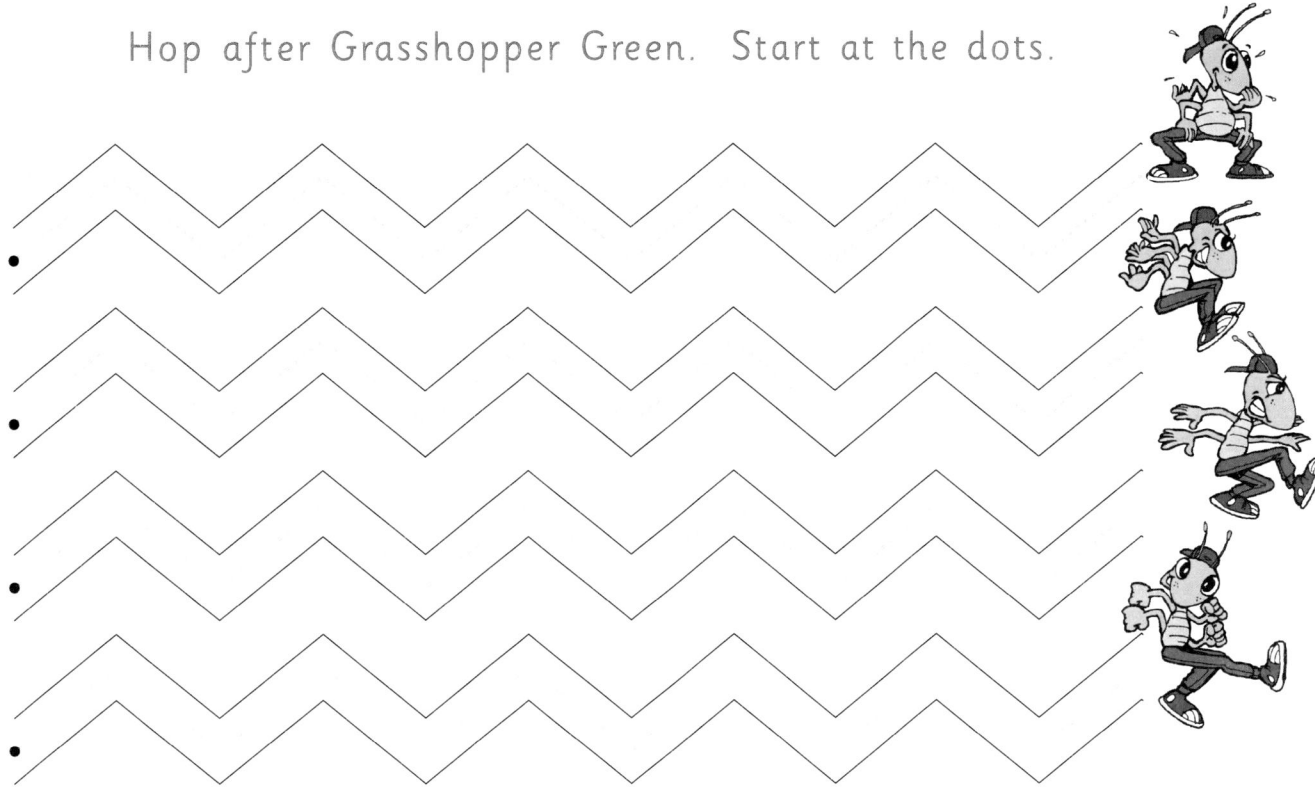

Follow Sally Snail's slimy trail. Start at the dots.

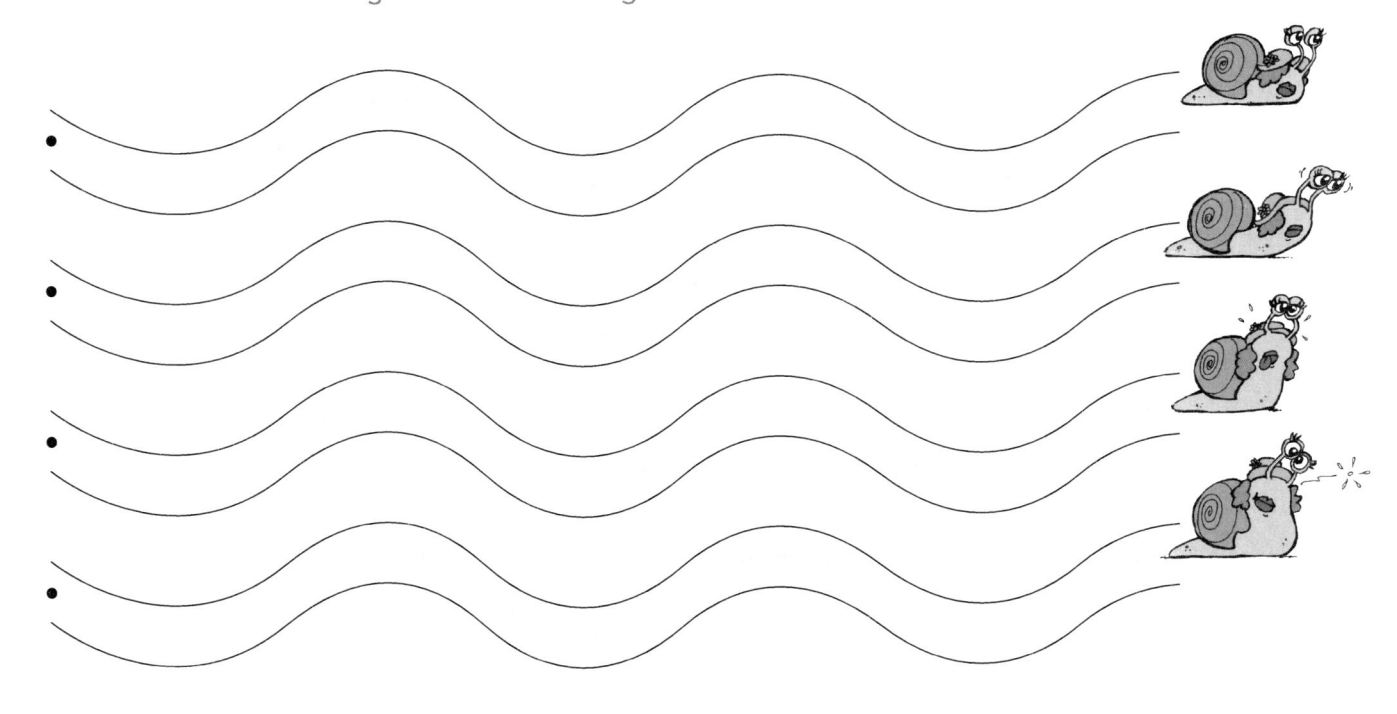

Top Tip: If the child needs more practice, try drawing lines on plain paper with a light-coloured, broad, felt tip pen. The child can use a pencil to trace over your lines. Make sure he or she always begins on the left.

Remember to line up the base of this icon with the edge of your table.

Remember to hold your pencil correctly.

STAGE 1 WORKSHEET 5

Slide down Sam Spider's cobwebs. Start at the dots.

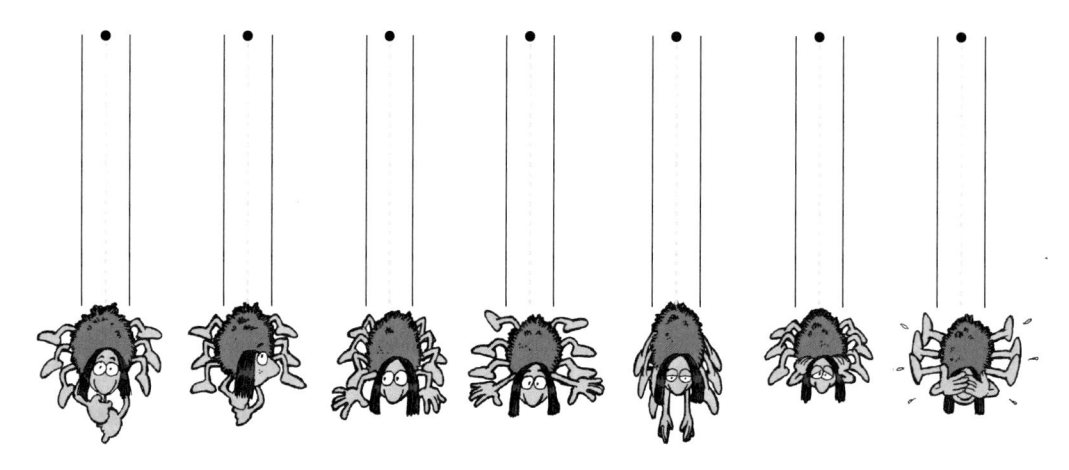

Follow Sam down the drainpipe. Start at the dots.

These drainpipes look like the letter 'l'.
Write some more 'l's. Start at the dots.

Grasshopper Green has been jumping across the page.
Hop with Grasshopper Green. Start at the dot.

Top Tip: *The child could practise making these shapes and patterns with their finger in a little dry sand or rice on a tray.*

Remember to line up the base of this icon with the edge of your table.

Remember to hold your pencil correctly.

STAGE 1 WORKSHEET 6

Billy Beetle is an insect.

Insect begins with an 'i'. Help Billy to make some 'i' letters. Start at the top of the letter and then do the dots.

Billy Beetle likes to eat jelly.

Jelly starts with a 'j'. Can you make some 'j' letters?

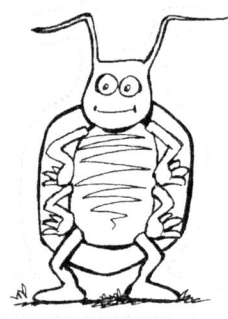

Can you draw round and colour Billy Beetle and the jelly?

Now follow Billy Beetle as he hunts for jelly. Remember to start at the dots.

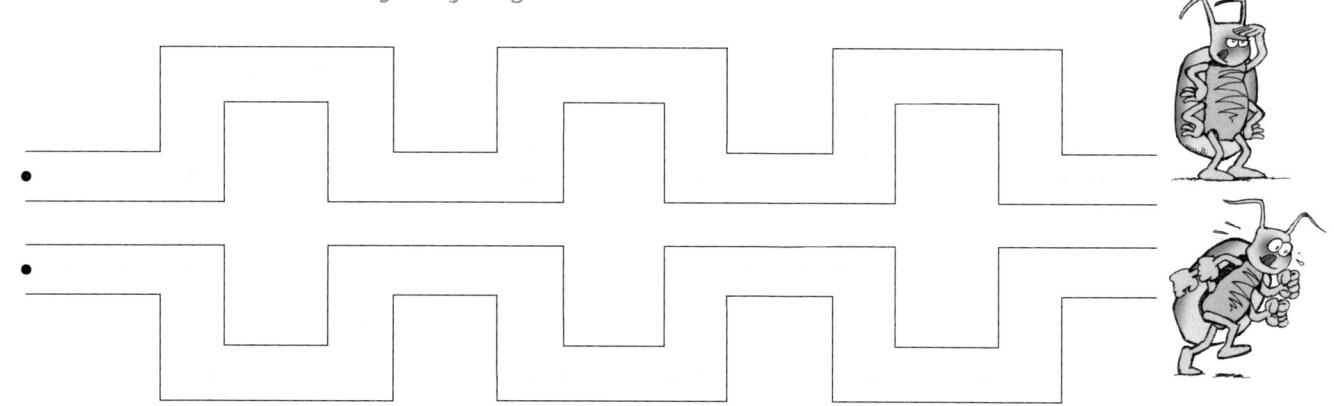

Top Tip: When the child is writing an 'i' or a 'j' it is helpful if they say "Top to bottom and then the dot." This helps them to get into the habit of adding the dot last.

Remember to line up the base of this icon with the edge of your table.

11

Remember to hold your pencil correctly. STAGE 1 WORKSHEET 7

Here is Charlie Caterpillar.
He has a very curly shape, like the letter 'c'.

Can you follow his curly body?
Start at the dot.

Draw the curly pattern on these snail shells. Start at the dots.

Now trace these curly 'c' letters.

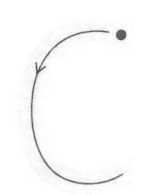

Some day, Charlie Caterpillar will turn into a beautiful butterfly.

Draw round this butterfly and then colour him with your crayons to make him beautiful.

Top Tip: *Colouring in helps to develop pencil control. Your child will need a lot of extra practice to get into the habit of writing anticlockwise letters. Try writing the letter 'c' – and the letters 'o' and 'e' from Worksheet 8 – in the air as well as on paper. A stick with a streamer on the end is great for this!*

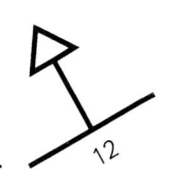

Remember to line up the base of this icon with the edge of your table.

Remember to hold your pencil correctly.

STAGE 1 WORKSHEET 8

Charlie has rolled into an 'o' shape.
Trace the 'o's. Start at the dots.

Charlie has been nibbling these leaves!
Draw round the holes that Charlie made.
Start at the dots.

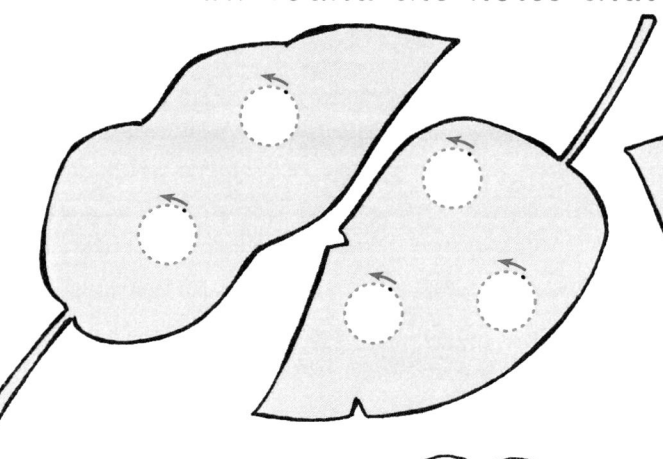

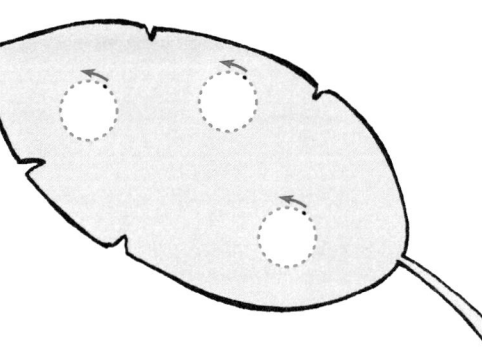

Charlie's head looks like a letter 'e'.
Trace the 'e'.
Start at the dot.

Now trace these 'e' letters.

Top Tip: In order for the child to develop a legible and fast-flowing handwriting style, it is vital that they get into the habit of making an 'o' in an anticlockwise direction. This can be harder for left-handers initially. When the child is writing an 'o', suggest they begin as if writing a 'c' and then complete the circle.

Remember to line up the base of this icon with the edge of your table.

Remember to hold your pencil correctly.

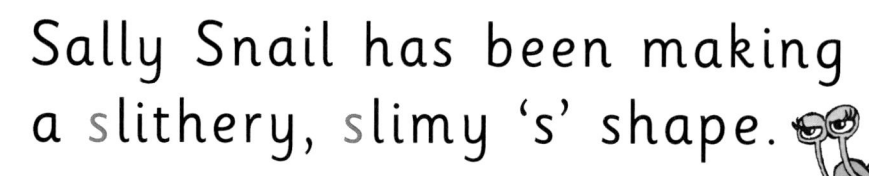

STAGE 1   WORKSHEET   9

Sally Snail has been making a slithery, slimy 's' shape.

Can you trace it? Start at the dot.

Now trace these slithery 's' letters.

Charlie Caterpillar has been making letter shapes in the garden.
Follow Sally Snail round the garden
and trace each letter you find.

Top Tip: *Encourage the child to trace the trail with their finger before they begin. Left-handers often need a lot of practice to train the brain to follow print from left to right. As you read to the child, run your finger under the print and encourage beginner readers to do the same.*

Remember to line up the base of this icon with the edge of your table.

14

Remember to hold your pencil correctly.

STAGE 1 WORKSHEET 10

Follow Grasshopper Green as he hops along. Start at the dot.

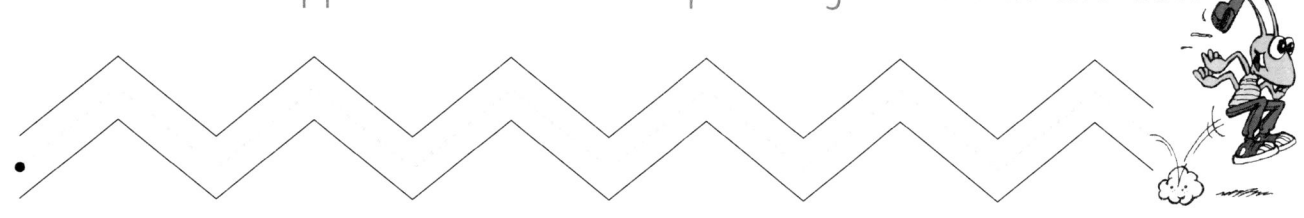

Grasshopper Green can make letter shapes as he jumps.

Make the letters 'v' and 'w' with Grasshopper Green. Start at the dots.

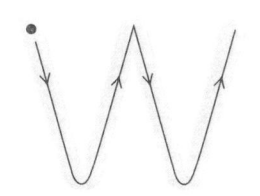

Now trace these letters. Start at the dots.

It is a very windy day.

Chase after Grasshopper Green and help him jump.

Top Tip: *Encourage the child to trace the large letters with their finger before using a pencil.*

Remember to line up the base of this icon with the edge of your table.

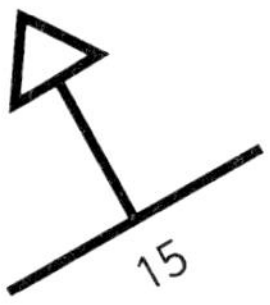

Remember to hold your pencil correctly.

STAGE 1 WORKSHEET 11

The flower bed has a very pretty border.
Can you trace its shape? Start at the dot.

Grasshopper Green is jumping again.
He is making a different letter shape now!
When he wants to race, he makes an 'r' shape.

Trace the 'r'. Start at the dot.
"Top to bottom. Up and over."

Grasshopper Green likes to race.
Now trace these letters. Start at the dots.

Now trace this pattern. Start at the dot.

Top Tip: To help the child get into the habit of starting these letters at the top, say as they write – "Top to bottom. Up and over." This helps to fix the pattern in the child's mind.

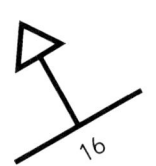

Remember to line up the base of this icon with the edge of your table.

Remember to hold your pencil correctly.

STAGE 1 WORKSHEET 12

Sam Spider has been making a cobweb. Can you help him? Trace over the lines.

Now trace over this 't' letter. Make sure you start at the top, go down to the end, lift your pencil off and then make the line across.

"Top to bottom. Then across."

Now trace these letters. Start at the dots.

Trace this wavy pattern. Start at the dot.

Top Tip: The letter 't' is the only lower case letter that is formed differently by left-handers. Right-handers cross the 't' from left to right. When left-handers develop a flowing, joined handwriting style, it is easier and quicker to cross the 't' from right to left when the word is complete. Encourage left-handers to cross 't's from right to left when learning to write.

Remember to line up the base of this icon with the edge of your table.

Remember to hold your pencil correctly.

STAGE 1 WORKSHEET 13

It's a rainy day in the garden, the wind is making waves in the pond.
Trace along the waves. Start at the dots.

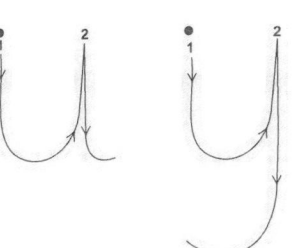

Help Sam Spider to make these letters. Start at the dots.

Now trace these letters.

Sam is climbing up the yellow tulips.
Trace the 'u' letters. Start at the dots!

Remember to line up the base of this icon with the edge of your table.

Top Tip: Ask at the child's setting if they have a letter formation handout.

Remember to hold your pencil correctly.

STAGE 1 WORKSHEET 14

Busy Bee likes apples and quinces.

a q

Trace the letters. Start at the dots.

She is visiting the apple and quince trees.

Now trace these letters. Start at the dots.

Busy Bee is flying around the apple and quince trees.
Follow Busy Bee and trace the letters you find. Start at the dots.

Top Tip: Lower case 'a's and 'q's are written in an anticlockwise direction. You could remind the child to begin as if writing a 'c' (curly caterpillar) – "Round, up to the top, and down again." Repeat it each time the child writes the letter.

Remember to line up the base of this icon with the edge of your table.

19

Remember to hold your pencil correctly.

STAGE 1 WORKSHEET 15

Busy Bee has been flying round and round.
Follow Busy Bee round and round. Start at the dot.

Busy Bee is getting dizzy and giddy.

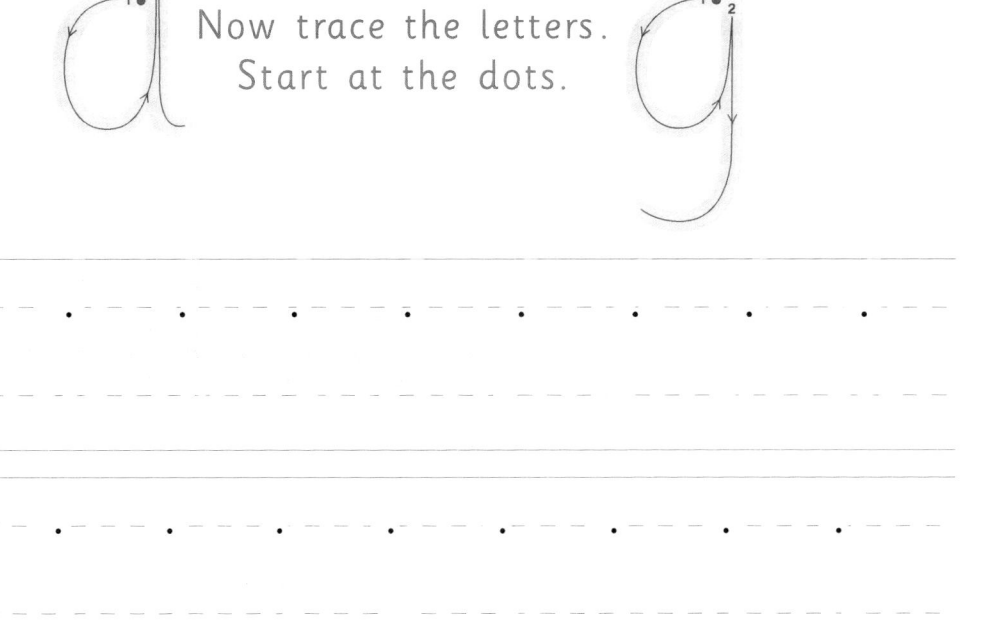

Now trace the letters. Start at the dots.

Trace Busy Bee's bee-lines. Start at the dots.

Top Tip: Lower case 'd's and 'g's are also written in an anticlockwise direction. Remind the child to begin as if writing a 'c' (curly caterpillar) – "Round, up to the top, and down again." Repeat this each time the child writes the letter.

Remember to line up the base of this icon with the edge of your table.

Remember to hold your pencil correctly.

STAGE 1 WORKSHEET 16

Billy Beetle likes to burrow.

Follow Billy Beetle along his burrow. Start at the dot.

Billy Beetle is making a burrow.

Trace the letter. Start at the dot.

Trace the letters. Start at the dots.

Top Tip: To help the child get into the habit of starting these letters at the top, say – as they write – "Top to bottom. Up and over." This helps to fix the pattern in the child's mind.

Remember to line up the base of this icon with the edge of your table.

Remember to hold your pencil correctly.

STAGE 1 WORKSHEET   17

Billy Beetle hops down a hill.

Trace over Billy Beetle's tracks. Start at the dots.

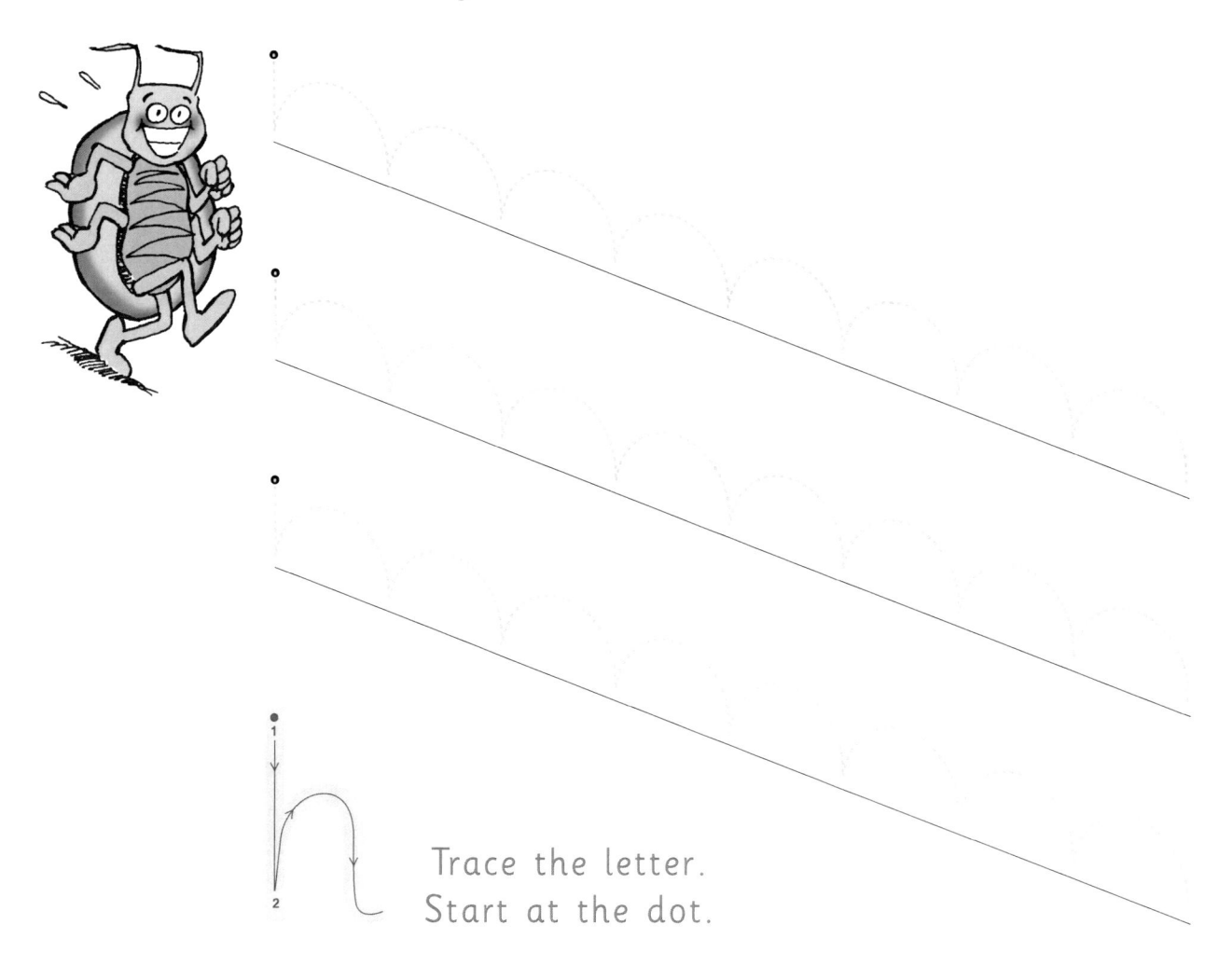

Trace the letter.
Start at the dot.

Now trace these letters. Start at the dots.

Top Tip: The child could practise letter formation using a bucket of water and a large paintbrush, writing on your patio or wall – if it's a sunny day!

Remember to line up the base of this icon with the edge of your table.

Remember to hold your pencil correctly.

STAGE 1 WORKSHEET 18

Willie Woodlouse has got lots of legs. He likes to play football.
Willie Woodlouse can kick.

Trace the letter.
Start at the dot.

Now trace these letters. Start at the dots.

Follow Willie Woodlouse as he kicks a ball around the garden.
Trace all the 'k' letters that you find.

Top Tip: *Encourage the child to trace over the path with their finger before they begin to write with their pencil.*

Remember to line up the base of this icon with the edge of your table.

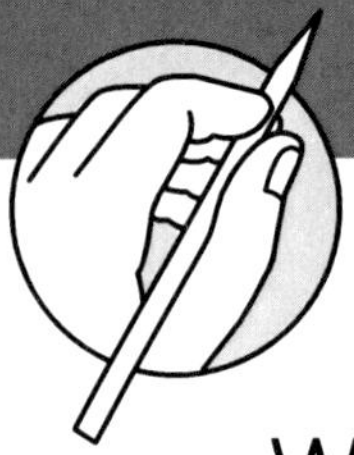

Remember to hold your pencil correctly.

STAGE 1 WORKSHEET 19

Willie Woodlouse has been on a long journey.
Help him find his way home. Start at the dot.

Willie Woodlouse has run out of puff.

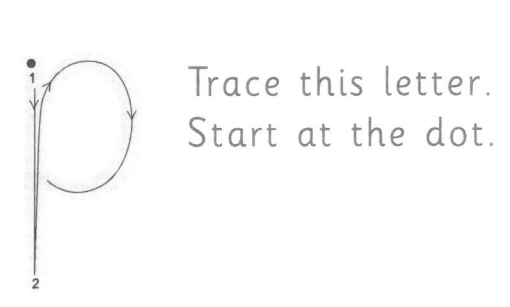

Trace this letter.
Start at the dot.

Trace the letters. Start at the dots.

Top Tip: *A white board and a dry wipe pen can be useful for the child to practise letter formation more extensively.*

Remember to line up the base of this icon with the edge of your table.

Remember to hold your pencil correctly.

STAGE 1 WORKSHEET 20

Willie lives in the flower bed.

Trace this letter.
Start at the dots.

Trace the flower stems. Start at the dots.

Now trace these letters. Start at the dots.

Top Tip: It is best to cross the 'f' from left to right because this will help when the child needs to join letters.

Remember to line up the base of this icon with the edge of your table.

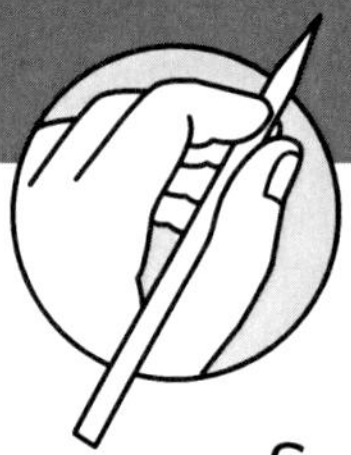

Remember to hold your pencil correctly.　　　　　　　　　　STAGE 1　WORKSHEET　　21

Sally Snail likes making crosses. She can make 'x' letters.

Trace this letter.
Start at the dots.

Now trace these letters. Start at the dots.

Sally Snail likes making zigzags.

Trace this letter.
Start at the dot.

Follow Sally Snail along her zigzag trails. Start at the dots.

Now trace these letters. Start at the dots.

Sally Snail has gone to sleep after all that writing!

Remember to line up the base of this icon with the edge of your table.

Top Tip: Ask at the child's setting about letter shapes used.

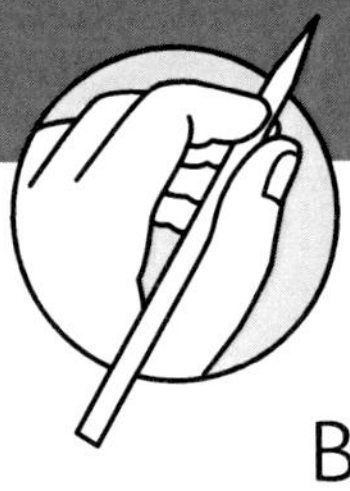

Remember to hold your pencil correctly.

STAGE 1 WORKSHEET 22

Busy Bee likes to count as she buzzes round the garden.
She has spotted Sally.

She counts one snail.

Trace the number.
Start at the dot.

Now trace these numbers. Start at the dots.

. . . .

Busy Bee counts four flowerpots.

Trace the number.
Start at the dots.

Now trace these numbers. Start at the dots.

. . . .

Top Tip: *Learning to write and practising each of the ten numbers will help the child with number recognition.*

Remember to line up the base of this icon with the edge of your table.

Remember to hold your pencil correctly.

STAGE 1 WORKSHEET 23

Busy Bee can count three butterflies fluttering.
Perhaps one was Charlie Caterpillar!

Trace the number.
Start at the dot.

Now trace these numbers. Start at the dots.

Busy Bee can see some strawberries.
She can count eight strawberries.

Trace the number.
Start at the dot.

Now trace these numbers. Start at the dots.

Top Tip: *Play 'Guess the number' with the child. Draw a number with your finger on the child's back and ask them to name it. Then let them draw a number on your back for you to guess!*

Remember to line up the base of this icon with the edge of your table.

Remember to hold your pencil correctly.

STAGE 1 WORKSHEET 24

Busy Bee buzzes over a blackbird's nest.
The nest is empty. All the eggs have hatched.

Trace the number.
Start at the dot.

0

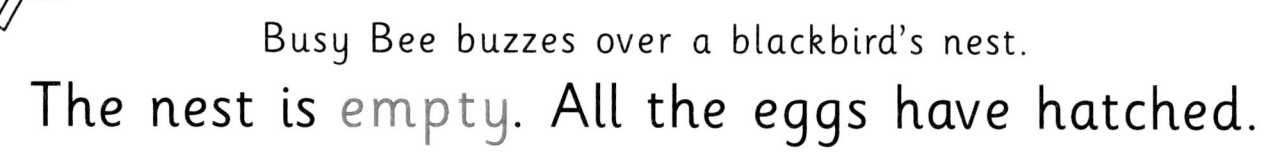

Now trace these numbers. Start at the dots.

Busy Bee can see Billy Beetle out for a walk with his family.
She can see six beetles.

Trace the number.
Start at the dot.

6

Now trace these numbers. Start at the dots.

Top Tip: Both these numbers are written in an anticlockwise direction. You might need to remind the child to begin by making a 'curly caterpillar shape'.

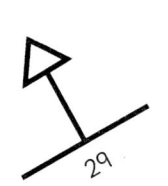

Remember to line up the base of this icon with the edge of your table.

Remember to hold your pencil correctly.

STAGE 1 WORKSHEET

Busy Bee sees some birds on the lawn.
She counts seven sparrows.

Trace the number.
Start at the dot.

7

Now trace these numbers. Start at the dots.

Busy Bee buzzes round the garden.
She can see a line of nine ants.

Trace the number.
Start at the dot.

9

Now trace these numbers. Start at the dots.

Top Tip: It is useful to practise number formation so that numbers can be written clearly and simply.

Remember to line up the base of this icon with the edge of your table.

Remember to hold your pencil correctly.

STAGE 1 WORKSHEET 26

Busy Bee can see two squirrels as she buzzes round the garden.

Trace the number.
Start at the dot.

2

Now trace these numbers. Start at the dots.

. . . .

Busy Bee is buzzing over the pond.
She can count five frogs.

Trace the number.
Start at the dot.

5

Now trace these numbers. Start at the dots.

. . . .

Top Tip: It is sometimes suggested that the number 5 is written in a downward direction, with the crossbar added afterwards. A left-hander may find it more comfortable to begin top right and follow the number shape. Both methods are acceptable.

Remember to line up the base of this icon with the edge of your table.

Remember to hold your pencil correctly.

STAGE 1 WORKSHEET 27

Follow Busy Bee round the garden.
Count all the things she sees and put the right number in each box.
Be sure to write the numbers carefully!

Top Tip: There are numbers all around us – on doors, car number plates, clocks, etc. Encourage the child to look for numbers and practise their shapes.

Remember to line up the base of this icon with the edge of your table.

32

Remember to hold your pencil correctly.　　　　　　　　　STAGE 1　WORKSHEET　28

Busy Bee has seen lots of things as she buzzes round the garden.
Write over these words.

quince
fox
shed
hive
weed
bug
lily
pot
mouse
pond
fish
rock
jar
lizard
gate

Top Tip: *Every letter has been included on this page. Watch the child's letter formation carefully, as they complete the words, to see if they need to practise any particular letters.*

Remember to line up the base of this icon with the edge of your table.

33

STAGE 1   REFERENCE SHEET

a b c d e
f g h i j k
l m n o p
q r s t u
v w x y z

Top Tip: Use this page as a handy reference for independent writing.

STAGE 1 REFERENCE SHEET

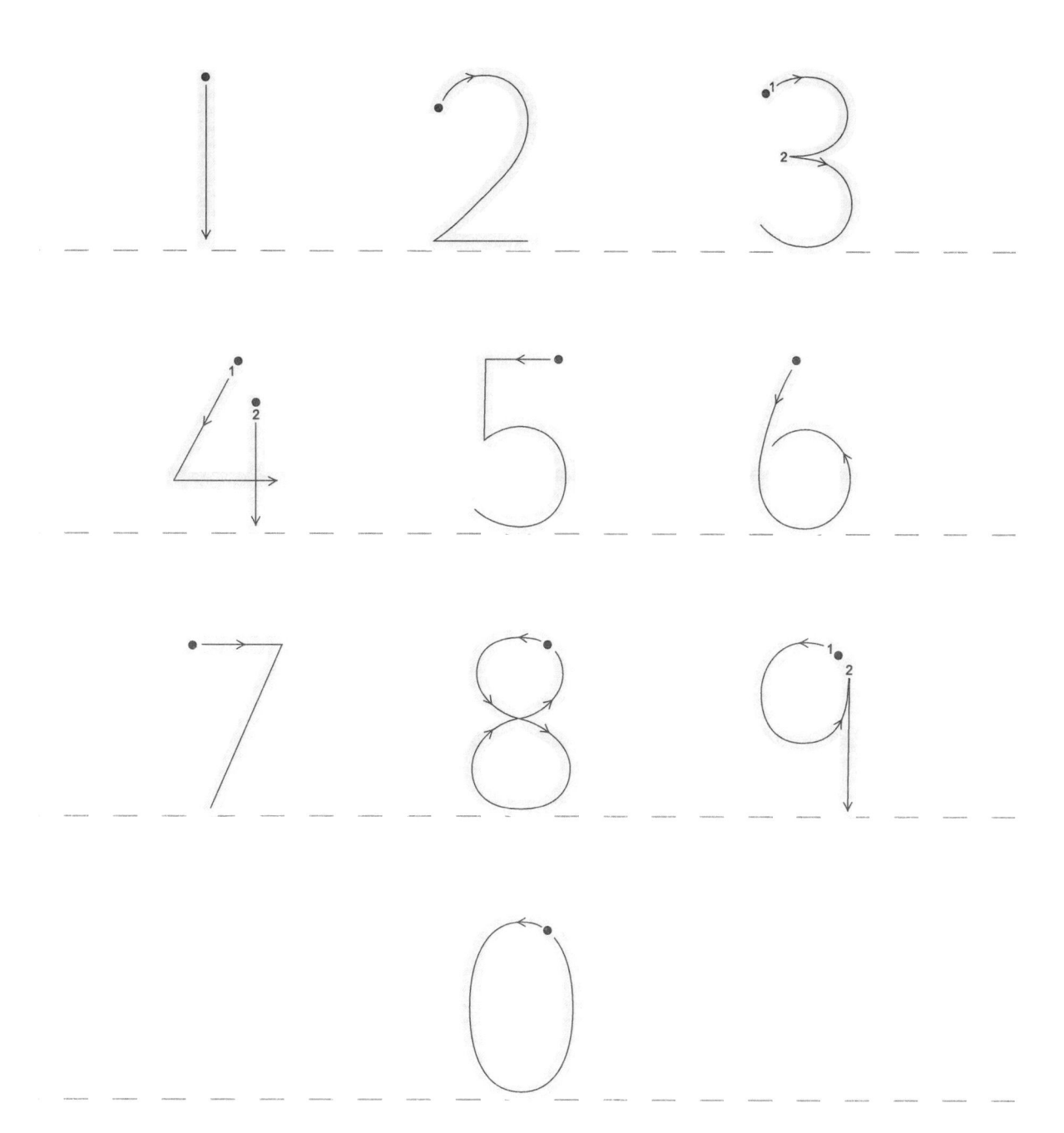

1 2 3

4 5 6

7 8 9

0

Top Tip: Use this page as a handy reference for independent writing.

Stage 2

funky formation and flaus

Remember to hold your pencil correctly.

STAGE 2 WORKSHEET 1

"Hi, I'm Pencil Pat and I'm going to help you become a really neat writer! So... get your fingers wriggling and try these patterns and letters to warm them up."

First, trace the pattern above.
Now trace these letters and then complete the row.
Always start at the dots.

i i i i i i i

j j j j j . . . . j

l l l l l l l

t t t t t . . . . t

u u u u . . . . u

Trace these letters.

Pencil Pat can...

look up

jump in

turn

Check this out!

1. For a flowing, joined handwriting style, it is easier for left-handers to cross their 't's from right to left.
2. Remember, all these letters start at the top and then the dots or cross are added afterwards.

Now trace this pattern.

Turn your paper clockwise. The base of this arrow icon should line up with the edge of your desk.

37

Remember to hold your pencil correctly.

STAGE 2 WORKSHEET 2

"Here are some more finger-wriggling patterns to try."

Trace the pattern. Start at the dot and do the whole row without taking your pencil off the paper.

All these letters start at the top and flow from left to right.
Trace these letters and then complete the row.

r r r r r   r

n n n n   n

m m m   m

Check this out!

Try to keep your letters all the same size and make them fit neatly between the lines.

Trace these letters. Pencil Pat can...

really make a muddle

and then make it neat.

Now trace this pattern.

Turn your paper clockwise. The base of this arrow icon should line up with the edge of your desk.

Remember to hold your pencil correctly.

STAGE 2 WORKSHEET 3

Pencil Pat and the gang are full of energy today.
Trace this pattern.

These letters start at the top and flow in a clockwise way.
Trace the letters and then complete the row.

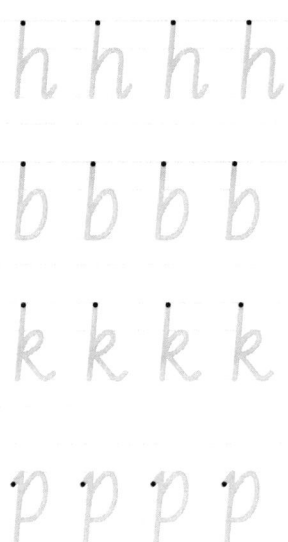

h h h h   h

b b b b   b

k k k k   k

p p p p   p

Check this out!

Are all your letters the same size?

bounce

pop

kick

Trace these bouncing letters.

hop

Now trace this pattern.

Turn your paper clockwise. The base of this arrow icon should line up with the edge of your desk.

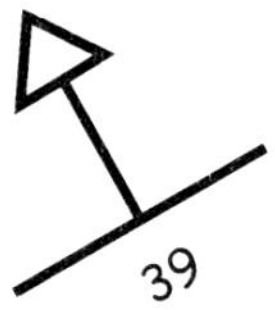

39

Remember to hold your pencil correctly.

STAGE 2 WORKSHEET 4

Trace the patterns and letters
as Pencil Pat gets ready to jump!

All these letters flow in an anticlockwise direction.
Trace the letters and then complete the row.

c c c c c   c

o o o o o   o

e e e e e   e

Trace these letters.

Pencil Pat...

easily   jump

can

over

Now trace this pattern.

Turn your paper clockwise. The base of this arrow icon should line up with the edge of your desk.

Remember to hold your pencil correctly.

STAGE 2 WORKSHEET 5

Pencil Pat and the gang like to draw. Do you?

Trace this pattern.

All these letters flow in an anticlockwise direction.
Trace the letters and then complete the row.

a a a a a   a

d d d d d   d

g g g g g   g

Pencil Pat and his buddies can...

doodle away

great

Trace these letters.

Now trace this pattern.

Turn your paper clockwise. The base of this arrow icon should line up with the edge of your desk.

Remember to hold your pencil correctly.

STAGE 2 WORKSHEET 6

"It's a challenge! Can you draw a square fish?
What would you call it?"

Trace this pattern.

All these letters begin in an anticlockwise direction.
Trace the letters and then complete the row.

q q q q q   q

f f f f f   f

s s s s s   s

Pencil Pat and his chums can...

draw a square fish

Trace these letters.

Now trace this pattern.

Turn your paper clockwise. The base of this arrow icon should line up with the edge of your desk.

42

STAGE 2 WORKSHEET 7

Remember to hold your pencil correctly.

Pencil Pat and the gang are keeping fit!
Exercise your fingers first by tracing these patterns!

All these letters have a zigzag shape. Trace and complete.

v v v v v v   v

w w w w   w

Pencil Pat and the team can...

walk
everywhere

Trace the letters.

Trace and complete.

x x x x x   x

y y y y y   y

z z z z z   z

Now trace these letters. **Pencil Pat can...**

play the xylophone
with zest.

Turn your paper clockwise. The base of this arrow icon should line up with the edge of your desk.

Remember to hold your pencil correctly.

STAGE 2 WORKSHEET 8

Are you ready for some funky stuff? Pencil Pat says: "It's time to begin joining up your letters."

First, trace this pattern.

Trace these letters and then complete the row.

ai

ai   ai

ar

ar   ar

Check this out!

Don't press down too hard — you might make a hole in the paper!

un

un   un

Now trace this pattern.

Turn your paper clockwise. The base of this arrow icon should line up with the edge of your desk.

44

Remember to hold your pencil correctly.

STAGE 2   WORKSHEET   9

"Don't get your fingers in a twist," says Pencil Pat.

Trace and copy these words.

air   lair   hair   pair

air   lair   hair   pair

Now trace this pattern.

Check this out!

Remember to cross the 't's from right to left!

Trace and copy these words.

bar   car   tar   ear

bar   car   tar   ear

Now trace this pattern.

"If you've got this far, you're doing really well!"

Turn your paper clockwise. The base of this arrow icon should line up with the edge of your desk.

45

Remember to hold your pencil correctly.

STAGE 2 WORKSHEET 10

Pencil Pat's pal is learning to play the guitar.

Do you know this song: 'Row, row, row your boat, gently down the stream.'? Try singing it slowly as you trace the patterns on this page!

A rhythm can help you get a nice writing flow.

Trace and copy these words.

bun   nun   sun   sung

bun   nun   sun   sung

Trace this pattern.

Trace and copy these words.

bump   hump   lump

bump   hump   lump

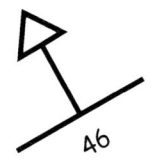

Now trace this pattern.

Turn your paper clockwise. The base of this arrow icon should line up with the edge of your desk.

Remember to hold your pencil correctly.

STAGE 2 WORKSHEET 11

"Get ready to make these letters join," says Pencil Pat.

First, trace the pattern.

Now trace and copy these letters.

ou

ou   ou

vi

vi   vi

wi

wi   wi

Check this out!

Don't hold your pen or pencil too tightly — it doesn't make your writing any better and your fingers will get tired.

Now trace this pattern.

Turn your paper clockwise. The base of this arrow icon should line up with the edge of your desk.

Remember to hold your pencil correctly.

STAGE 2 WORKSHEET 12

Pencil Pat and his crew are fishing.

Trace and copy these words.

or   rod   row   vow

or   rod   row   vow

"Have a go at these exercises —
but don't rock the boat!"

First, trace this pattern.

Check this out!

Try to keep your letters all the same size and make them fit neatly between the lines.

Now trace and copy these letter patterns.

acacacacacacacacacaca

unununununununununun

Turn your paper clockwise. The base of this arrow icon should line up with the edge of your desk.

Remember to hold your pencil correctly.

STAGE 2 WORKSHEET 13

Hop your fingers along with Pencil Pat as you trace and copy these words.

First, trace this pattern.

Trace and copy these words.

big   pig   dog   log

bow   cow   sun   bun

pin   tin   hop   mop

Pencil Pat likes playing with words.

Now trace this pattern.

Turn your paper clockwise. The base of this arrow icon should line up with the edge of your desk.

Remember to hold your pencil correctly.

STAGE 2 WORKSHEET 14

Pencil Pat and the gang are busily drawing patterns. You can practice the patterns in this book using the Practice Sheet on page 96.

Trace this pattern.

Check this out!

For a flowing, joined handwriting style, it is easier for left-handers to cross their 't's from right to left.

Trace and copy these letters.

ab

ab   ab

ul

ul   ul

it

it   it

Now trace this pattern.

"Gosh!" Pencil Pat says. "You are halfway through this stage now — and you're doing very well. Keep it up!"

Turn your paper clockwise. The base of this arrow icon should line up with the edge of your desk.

Remember to hold your pencil correctly.

STAGE 2 WORKSHEET 15

"These patterns should make your fingers dizzy,"
says Pencil Pat!

Trace and copy these words with Pencil Pat and his posse.

dab   nab   pull   bull

dab   nab   pull   bull

"Be careful! That bull looks angry, Pencil Pat!"

bit   hit   lit   sit

bit   hit   lit   sit

Check this out!

Remember to cross the 't's and dot the 'i's at the end of each word.

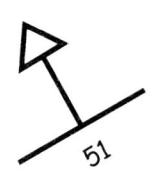

Now trace this pattern.

Turn your paper clockwise. The base of this arrow icon should line up with the edge of your desk.

Remember to hold your pencil correctly.

STAGE 2 WORKSHEET 16

Pencil Pat and the gang all have different hobbies. Guess which clubs they belong to.

Trace this pattern.

Check this out!

Try to keep your letters all the same size and make them fit between the lines.

Now trace and copy these words.

hat   bat   cut   nut

hat   bat   cut   nut

Trace and copy these letter patterns.

lblblblblblblblblblbl

hlhlhlhlhlhlhlhlhlhl

Turn your paper clockwise. The base of this arrow icon should line up with the edge of your desk.

52

Remember to hold your pencil correctly.

STAGE 2 WORKSHEET 17

Pencil Pat's friends are enjoying practising their writing!

Trace this pattern.

Now join these letters up with Pencil Pat's buddies.
Trace and copy the letters.

ot

ot ot

wh

wh wh

ot

ot ot

Now trace these patterns.

Check this out!

Remember not to press down too hard or hold your pencil too tightly.

Turn your paper clockwise. The base of this arrow icon should line up with the edge of your desk.

Remember to hold your pencil correctly.

STAGE 2 WORKSHEET 18

Pencil Pat and the group are having fun!

Trace and copy these words with Pencil Pat's friends.
As you trace the patterns, say the words 'old, cold, hot, pot,
old, cold, hot, pot' in time with your writing.

Check this out!

Remember to cross the 't's from right to left!

old cold hot pot

old cold hot pot

Now trace these patterns.

Trace and copy these words.

wham   *whack*

wham   *whack*

Turn your paper clockwise. The base of this arrow icon should line up with the edge of your desk.

STAGE 2 WORKSHEET 19

Remember to hold your pencil correctly.

It's quiz time. Pencil Pat and the gang are making their brains work hard today!

Trace and copy these question words with Pencil Pat's puzzled pals.

why?   who?   what?

why?   who?   what?

Check this out!

Are all your letters the same size and do they fit neatly between the lines?

Now trace this mad pattern.

Trace and copy these letter patterns.

whwhwhwhwhwh

olololololololololololol

Turn your paper clockwise. The base of this arrow icon should line up with the edge of your desk.

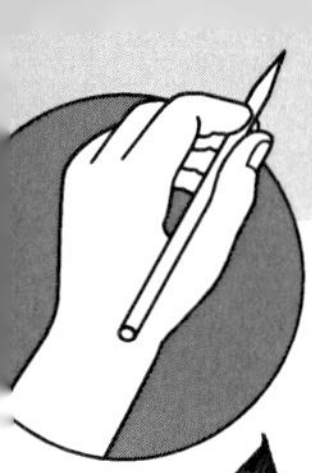

Remember to hold your pencil correctly.

STAGE 2 WORKSHEET 20

"Look before you leap, Pencil Pat.
Then maybe you won't end up in a puddle!"

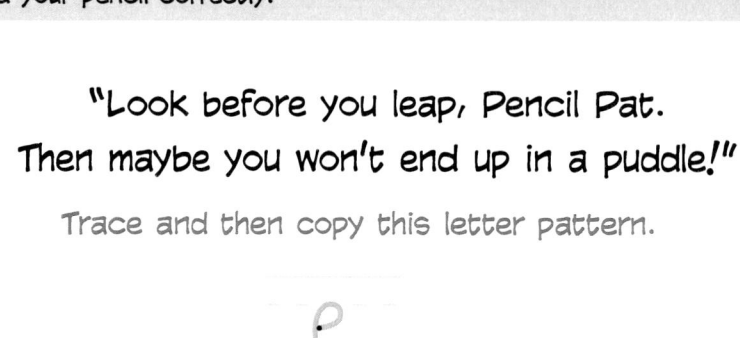

Trace and then copy this letter pattern.

e

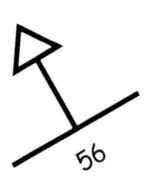

eeeeeeeeeeeeeeeeeeee

Trace and copy these words.

leg   leap   heap

leg   leap   heap

Now trace this pattern.

Trace and copy.

web   well   wet

web   well   wet

Turn your paper clockwise. The base of this arrow icon should line up with the edge of your desk.

Remember to hold your pencil correctly.

STAGE 2 WORKSHEET 21

Pencil Pat's troupe are putting on a circus show!

Trace and copy these letters.

rr rl

rrrlrrrlrrrlrrrlrrrlrrrl

Trace and copy these words.

circus ring

hurtle

Check this out!

Remember to cross the 't's from right to left!

Where did Pat find that turtle?

turtle

Now trace this pattern.

Turn your paper clockwise. The base of this arrow icon should line up with the edge of your desk.

Remember to hold your pencil correctly.

STAGE 2 WORKSHEET 22

Pencil Pat and the others are treasure-hunting. What have they found?

Trace and copy these letter patterns.

re

rerererererererere

Trace and copy these words.

treasure *trove*

seashore *shell*

Pencil Pat has a map and is ready to dig for treasure.

Now trace this pattern.

Turn your paper clockwise. The base of this arrow icon should line up with the edge of your desk.

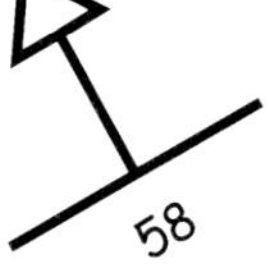

58

Remember to hold your pencil correctly.

STAGE 2 WORKSHEET 23

Pencil Pat says:
"Look carefully — some of these letters don't join!"

Trace and copy these letters.

jo   yo   go

jyg jyg jyg jyg jyg jyg jyg

Trace and copy these words.

jogging   jaguar

yellow   jelly

Pencil Pat says: "Never try to run with a jelly!"

Turn your paper clockwise. The base of this arrow icon should line up with the edge of your desk.

Remember to hold your pencil correctly.

STAGE 2 WORKSHEET 24

Today, Pencil Pat has gone to the beach with his mates.

Trace and complete these letters.

ff

Cross the 'ff's at the end of each pair.

ff ff ff ff ff ff ff ff ff ff

Now write your own 'ff's.

Trace and copy these words.

puffer   *fish*   *surf*

Check this out!

Look carefully — some of the letters don't join.

Pencil Pat is a bit squeamish about squid.

Trace and copy these words.

q

squirming   *squid*

Turn your paper clockwise. The base of this arrow icon should line up with the edge of your desk.

60

Remember to hold your pencil correctly.

STAGE 2 WORKSHEET 25

Look out! Here are some more tricky letter joins.

Trace and copy these letter patterns and words.

ozo   oxi

zzzzzzzzzzzzzzzzzzz

Check this out!

Look carefully — some of the letters don't join.
For extra practice, use the Practice Sheet on page 96.

Trace and copy these words.

zany   zebras

Pencil Pat — don't tear that zebra suit!

boxing   foxes

Now trace this pattern.

Well done — you have finished all the joins!

Turn your paper clockwise. The base of this arrow icon should line up with the edge of your desk.

Remember to hold your pencil correctly.

STAGE 2 WORKSHEET 26

IT'S PARTY TIME! All of Pencil Pat's friends are here to join the gang for a party.

Write these CAPITAL letters.
Check out CAPITAL letter formation on page 66.
Trace and copy each friend's name.

F   E   L

Fred   Emma   Liam

I   T   A

Ivor   Tara   Ali

M   N   V

Mark   Nick   Val

Pencil Pat has lots more friends for you to meet…

Turn your paper clockwise. The base of this arrow icon should line up with the edge of your desk.

62

Remember to hold your pencil correctly.

STAGE 2 WORKSHEET 27

"Here are some more of my mates.
Yes, even the dog has come to my party!"

Write these CAPITAL letters.
Trace and copy each friend's name.

W   H   K

Wilf   Holly   Kyle

X   Y   Z

Xenia   Yasmin   Zack

B   D   P

Ben   Daisy   Paul

"Who else is coming to the party?"

Turn your paper clockwise. The base of this arrow icon should line up with the edge of your desk.

Remember to hold your pencil correctly.

STAGE 2 WORKSHEET 28

Here are the rest of Pencil Pat's friends ready to join the fun!

Write these CAPITAL letters.
Trace and copy each friend's name.

R   C   G

Rob   Chloe   Gus

O   Q   S

Omar   Queeny   Sam

J   U

Josh   Una

Hurray! Well done!
You've made it to the end of this stage.

Turn your paper clockwise. The base of this arrow icon should line up with the edge of your desk.

STAGES 2 AND 3   REFERENCE SHEET

Check this out!

Use this page as a handy reference for independent writing.

a b c d e
f g h i j k
l m n o p
q r s t u
v w x y z

STAGES 2 AND 3   REFERENCE SHEET

Check this out!

Use this page as a handy reference for independent writing.

A B C D
E F G H I
J K L M N
O P Q R S
T U V W
X Y Z

66

Stage 3

successful
smudge-free
writing

1. Hold your pen correctly. 2. Keep your wrist straight. 3. Don't hold too tight!

STAGE 3
WORKSHEET 1

Come with us on a writing journey.
We're going to start in the Stone Age.

Begin by checking your letter formation.

Write over each letter.

a b c d e f g h i j k l m

n o p q r s t u v w x y z

A B C D E F G H I J K L M

N O P Q R S T U V W X Y Z

If you are not sure how to form any of these letters,
check on the letter formation pages 65 and 66.

Did you know?
The first kind of writing was in the form of pictures. We call these 'pictograms'.

Turn your paper clockwise. The base of this arrow icon should line up with the edge of your desk.

1. Hold your pen correctly. 2. Keep your wrist straight. 3. Don't hold too tight!

STAGE 3 WORKSHEET 2

There are four basic letter joins. We will look at these in turn.

This join runs from the base of a letter on the lower dotted line to the next letter at the upper dotted line.

Letter Join 1

ai   ar   un   ur   ir

Trace and complete this letter pattern.

ccccccccccccccc

Trace and copy these words.

big   pig   dig

mad   bad   lad

Trace and complete this letter pattern.

cacacacacacaca

Did you know?
The first ever written words were recorded in Iraq about 5,000 years ago!

The first words were scratched onto wet clay tablets which were then left to dry.

Turn your paper clockwise. The base of this arrow icon should line up with the edge of your desk.

1. Hold your pen correctly. 2. Keep your wrist straight. 3. Don't hold too tight!

STAGE 3
WORKSHEET 3

There are four basic letter joins

Letter Join 2

This join starts and finishes on the upper dotted line.

ou   ov   vi   wi   wo

Trace and complete this letter pattern.

oooooooooooooooooooo

Trace and copy these words.

ox   won   wow

These words use joins 1 and 2. Trace and copy them carefully.

cross   crow   cawing

Trace and complete this letter pattern.

ococococococococococ

Did you know? The Egyptians developed a form of pictogram writing called hieroglyphs about 5,000 years ago.

Turn your paper clockwise. The base of this arrow icon should line up with the edge of your desk.

70

STAGE 3
WORKSHEET 4

1. Hold your pen correctly.   2. Keep your wrist straight.   3. Don't hold too tight!

Letter Join 3

This join links the base of a letter to a tall letter.

ab   ut   it   th   bl

Trace and complete this letter pattern.

blblblblblblbl

Trace and copy these words.

all   elk   ebb

These words use joins 1, 2 and 3. Trace and copy them carefully.

slippery   slope   slide

Trace and complete this letter pattern.

ulululululululul

Writing developed in different ways all over the world.

Did you know? The Mayan People of Central America developed a pictogram system of their own between 300 and 900 A.D.

Turn your paper clockwise. The base of this arrow icon should line up with the edge of your desk.

1. Hold your pen correctly.   2. Keep your wrist straight.   3. Don't hold too tight!

STAGE 3
WORKSHEET 5

The Chinese invented paper.

Letter Join 4

This join begins on the upper dotted line, linking one letter to a tall letter.

ot   rt   ob   rk   wl

Trace and complete this letter pattern.

rkrkrkrkrkrk

These words use joins 1, 2 and 4. Trace and copy them carefully.

howl   bark   whine

Have a go at completing these patterns.

Did you know?
The Arabs learnt the secret of paper-making from Chinese prisoners of war in 168 A.D.

* Aiya!

Turn your paper clockwise. The base of this arrow icon should line up with the edge of your desk.

1. Hold your pen correctly. 2. Keep your wrist straight. 3. Don't hold too tight!

STAGE 3
WORKSHEET 6

Here are some special joins.

The letter 'f' is never joined from the letter before it.
The crossbar of the 'f' joins to the next letter... unless it's an 'e'.

Trace and copy these words.

fry   flat   fish   fetch   feast

Go on, try saying these words quickly!

Did you know? An octopus squirts ink when it is alarmed.

When there are two letter 'f's together,
write them both then add the cross bar.

fluffy   puffin

When an 'f' is followed by a 't'
join the 'f' to the 't'
and then add the cross bar to the 't'
after you've finished writing the word.

ft

I wonder if anyone has ever tried writing with octopus ink!

Trace and copy this sentence.

The life raft drifted after the ship.

Turn your paper clockwise. The base of this arrow icon should line up with the edge of your desk.

1. Hold your pen correctly.   2. Keep your wrist straight.   3. Don't hold too tight!

STAGE 3
WORKSHEET 7

Here are some more special joins.

The letter 'z' is never joined from the letter before it, but it does join to the next letter.

ze

Copy and trace these words.

zany   zebras   dozing   lazily

The letters 'g', 'j', 'q', 'y' and 'x' can be joined from the letter before them, but they don't like to join the next letter.
It's best to take your pen or pencil off the paper when you've written one of these letters and then begin the next letter.

go   jo   qu   xi   yo

Copy and trace these words.

squirming   jellyfish   giggling   foxes

Did you know?
Before paper was invented, people wrote on stones, pottery, bamboo, reeds and even animal skin.

Turn your paper clockwise. The base of this arrow icon should line up with the edge of your desk.

STAGE 3 WORKSHEET 8

1. Hold your pen correctly. 2. Keep your wrist straight. 3. Don't hold too tight!

The Chinese
developed a writing system all of their own.

Trace and copy the menu.

THE BAMBOO GARDEN MENU

STARTER
Chicken Noodle Soup

MAIN COURSE
Vegetable Chow Mein

Crispy Prawn Crackers

DESSERT
Pineapple Fritter

Did you know? Chinese characters are written one underneath the other in columns.

Turn your paper clockwise. The base of this arrow icon should line up with the edge of your desk.

STAGE 3
WORKSHEET 9

1. Hold your pen correctly. 2. Keep your wrist straight. 3. Don't hold too tight!

CHINESE WRITING is made up of characters that stand for a word or idea rather than a single letter. Each character is made up of as many as 26 different strokes which must be written in the correct order. Phew!

Did you know? There are over 50,000 Chinese characters!

Now write your own international menu. Choose any food you like.

Starter:

Tomato Soup

Garlic Bread

Chocolate Mousse

Melon

Baked Beans

Main Course:

Peas

Rice

Treacle Tart

Strawberry Ice Cream

Dessert:

Spaghetti Bolognaise   Chicken Curry   Chips   Cheese and Tomato Pizza

Turn your paper clockwise. The base of this arrow icon should line up with the edge of your desk.

76

STAGE 3
WORKSHEET 10

1. Hold your pen correctly. 2. Keep your wrist straight. 3. Don't hold too tight!

The first alphabet was used around 2000 B.C.
This alphabet developed into all the alphabets used today.
There are lots of different alphabets,
for example, Roman, Greek and Cyrillic
(which the Russian alphabet is based upon).

Trace and copy these Latin phrases and their meanings.
How many do you know?

Vice versa – the other way round

Terra firma – solid ground

TERRA VERY FIRMA !

Ad infinitum – endlessly

Did you know?
The alphabet we use for English is the Roman alphabet. The Ancient Romans used it for their Latin language.

Turn your paper clockwise. The base of this arrow icon should line up with the edge of your desk.

1. Hold your pen correctly. 2. Keep your wrist straight. 3. Don't hold too tight!

STAGE 3 WORKSHEET 11

Caesar and Calphurnia have been shopping at the market place.
Below are all the things they bought.
Trace Caesar's list
and then write the rest of the items on Calphurnia's list.

CAESAR **CALPHURNIA**

Olives

Toga

Sandals

Wine

Fish

Grapes

Complete the pattern above.

TURN YOUR PAPER CLOCKWISE. THE BASE OF THIS ARROW ICON SHOULD LINE UP WITH THE EDGE OF YOUR DESK.

STAGE 3 WORKSHEET 12

1. Hold your pen correctly. 2. Keep your wrist straight. 3. Don't hold too tight!

IN MEDIEVAL TIMES MANY PEOPLE COULD NOT READ OR WRITE. PEOPLE WHO WERE EMPLOYED TO WRITE WERE CALLED SCRIBES.

Did you know?
Until printing was invented in the 15th Century every book had to be written by hand!

Trace and copy this letter.

My dearest Guinevere,

Thank thee kindly for the

woolly socks knitted by

thine own fair hand.

from thy true love,
Sir Spearalot

Did you know?
Scribes used crushed beetles to make red ink!

FREEDOM FOR BEETLES

Complete this pattern.

Turn your paper clockwise. The base of this arrow icon should line up with the edge of your desk.

STAGE 3 WORKSHEET 13

1. Hold your pen correctly. 2. Keep your wrist straight. 3. Don't hold too tight!

Medieval scribes wrote with large bird feathers called quills.

Did you know?
Bird feathers curve – which means the feathers from the right wing of a large bird are best for left-handers!

HANDS OFF MY FEATHERS!!!

Now write your own letter.
Use the words around the page or your own ideas.
Try to use every line.

Dear

Words around the page:
- Uncle Bill
- Sybil
- I'm writing to ask
- if you would like to
- come swimming
- go to a party
- Mr Brown
- Thank you for
- the nice jumper
- the computer game
- the chocolates
- Let's meet at half-past two
- from
- Did you enjoy your holiday?
- It's great!
- Yours sincerely,
- See you soon.
- With lots of love,
- With best wishes,

Turn your paper clockwise. The base of this arrow icon should line up with the edge of your desk.

STAGE 3 WORKSHEET 14

1. Hold your pen correctly. 2. Keep your wrist straight. 3. Don't hold too tight!

THE CELTS WERE TRIBAL PEOPLE FROM THE EARLY MIDDLE AGES. THEY ARE MOST REMEMBERED FOR THEIR BEAUTIFUL ILLUMINATED MANUSCRIPTS. SOME CAN STILL BE SEEN IN MUSEUMS TODAY.

Copy this rhyme.

Arthur was a Celtic King,

The Anglo-Saxons feared him.

He battled with his fearless knights,

Who scattered all against them.

Did you know? Illuminated means the writing is decorated in gold and other colours. The Celts added extra pictures and designs to their writing.

Trace and complete this letter pattern.

urururururur

Turn your paper clockwise. The base of this arrow icon should line up with the edge of your desk.

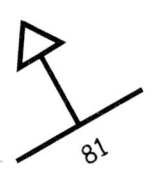

1. Hold your pen correctly. 2. Keep your wrist straight. 3. Don't hold too tight!

STAGE 3
WORKSHEET

Try some Celtic writing of your own...

Tape two pencils together so that the left is slightly shorter than the right.
(If your right-handed friends want to do this they will have to do it
the other way round.)

Try writing some large round letters.

Join the 'loose' ends and colour in with a black pen.
Try adding some spirals.

Here is Pat's name.
Finish the pattern around his name.

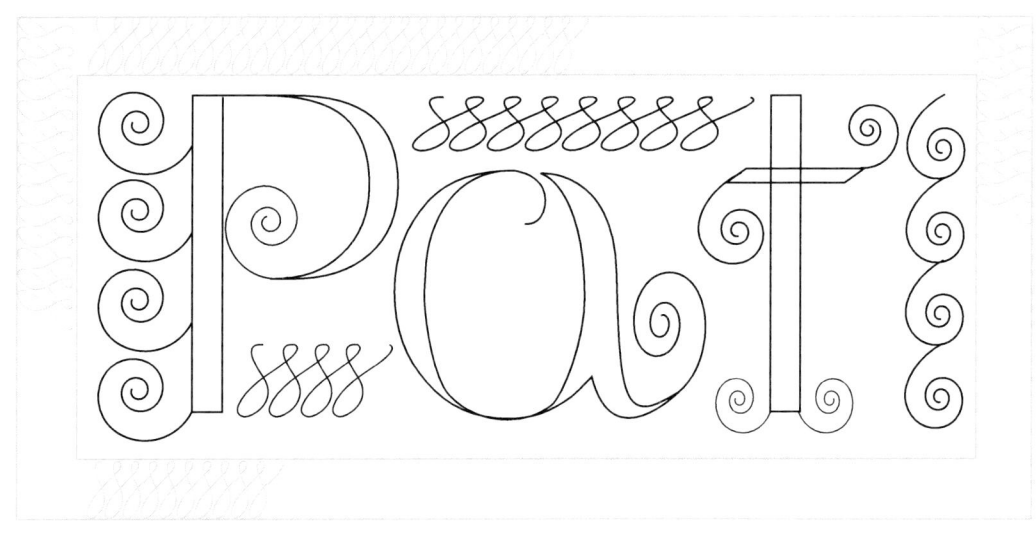

Now try writing your own name in a Celtic script.
If you use a piece of card, you could make it into a label for your door!

Turn your paper clockwise. The base of this arrow icon should line up with the edge of your desk.

STAGE 3
WORKSHEET 16

1. Hold your pen correctly. 2. Keep your wrist straight. 3. Don't hold too tight!

Copy this invitation.

The Court of King John

cordially invites thee

to the feast of St Stephen.

Bring thine own platter.

Did you know?
Envelopes weren't used until the 19th Century. Before then, letters were simply folded up and sometimes sealed with sealing wax.

Copy this letter pattern.

aeaeaeae

Turn your paper clockwise. The base of this arrow icon should line up with the edge of your desk.

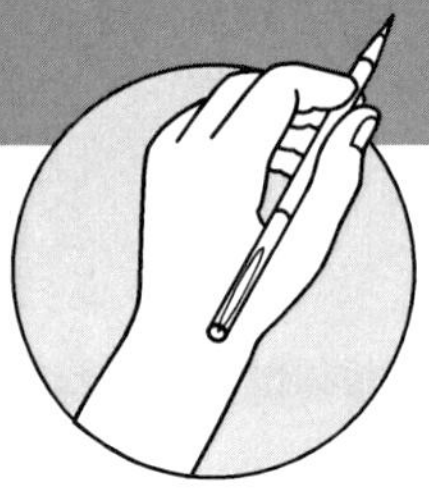

1. Hold your pen correctly. 2. Keep your wrist straight. 3. Don't hold too tight!

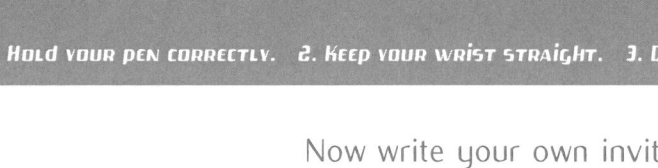

STAGE 3
WORKSHEET 17

Now write your own invitation.
Use the words around the page to help you, or write your own ideas.

Name

Would like to invite

Name

To a

On

Please

RSVP

On Friday 31st October   Please bring a pumpkin
To a birthday party
          Please wear smart clothes  
          On Saturday 12th August   To a Halloween party

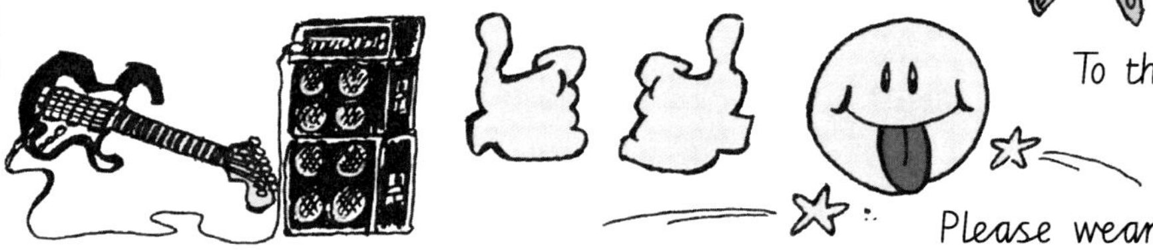

Mr and Mrs Brown   To the wedding of

                                                Please wear fancy dress

Did you know? RSVP is a French abbreviation: 'Répondez s'il vous plaît' which means 'please reply'.

Complete this pattern.

Turn your paper clockwise. The base of this arrow icon should line up with the edge of your desk.

84

1. Hold your pen correctly. 2. Keep your wrist straight. 3. Don't hold too tight!

STAGE 3 WORKSHEET

Copy this recipe.

Ye old recipe – Mutton Stew

Heat potful of stock on fire.

Add pieces of raw mutton.

Toss in sprigs of rosemary.

Add flagon of cider.

Simmer all morning.

Serve on a platter.

Turn your paper clockwise. The base of this arrow icon should line up with the edge of your desk.

STAGE 3 WORKSHEET 19

1. Hold your pen correctly. 2. Keep your wrist straight. 3. Don't hold too tight!

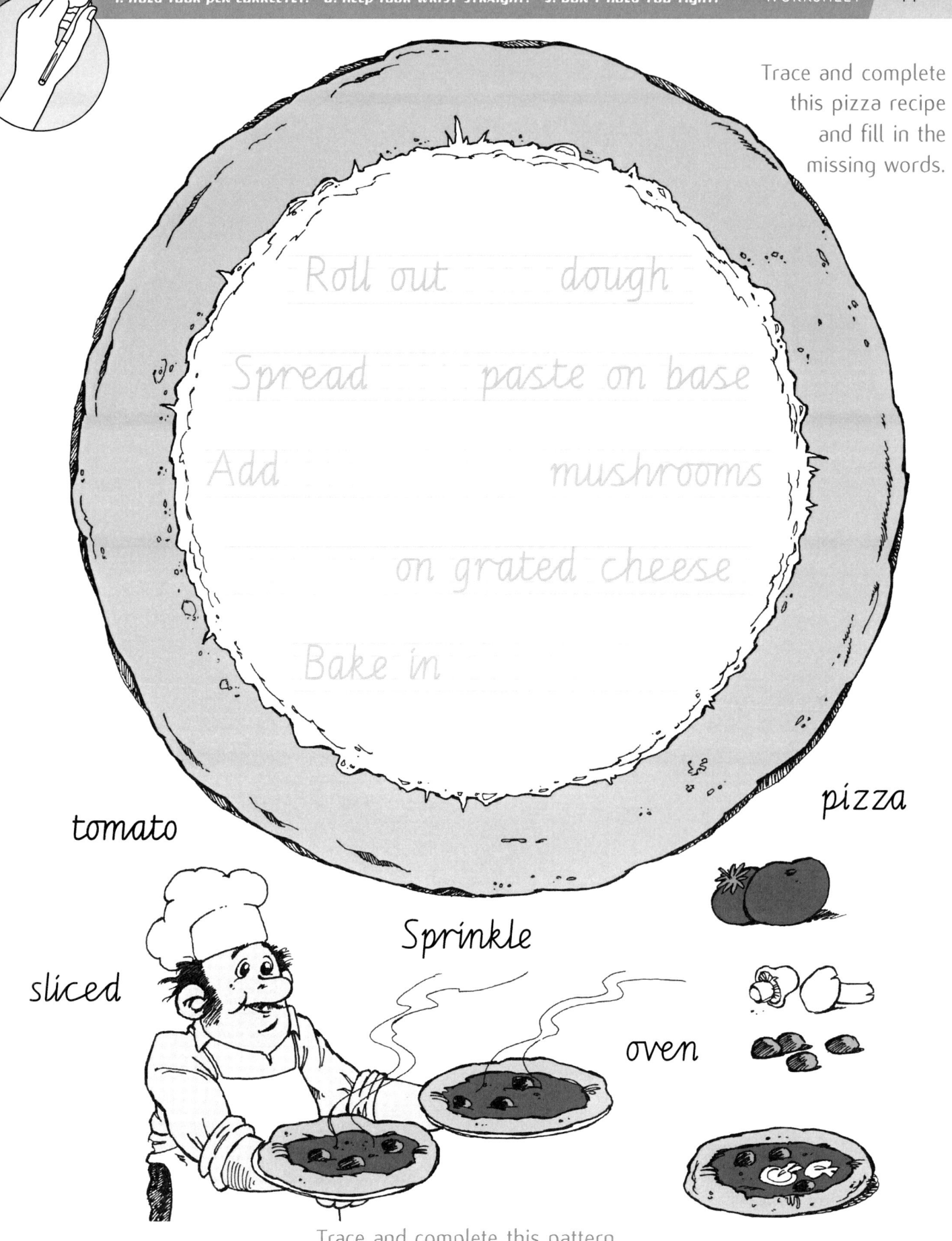

Trace and complete this pizza recipe and fill in the missing words.

Roll out _____ dough

Spread _____ paste on base

Add _____ mushrooms

_____ on grated cheese

Bake in _____

pizza

tomato

Sprinkle

sliced

oven

Trace and complete this pattern.

kekeke

Turn your paper clockwise. The base of this arrow icon should line up with the edge of your desk.

1. Hold your pen correctly. 2. Keep your wrist straight. 3. Don't hold too tight!

STAGE 3 WORKSHEET 20

Leonardo da Vinci was a 15th century artist and inventor. He is a famous left-hander. He wrote many of his notes in 'mirror-writing' (starting at the right and writing backwards towards the left hand side of the page).

Did you know?
Arabic is written from the right hand side to the left.

Someone has been to Paris. Can you read who?
Trace and copy his postcard.

Dear Joe

Yesterday, I went to the Louvre.

I saw the Mona Lisa.

See you soon, Leonardo.

Did you know? Some left-handers are good at mirror-writing. It's a good way of making your diary difficult for other people to read.

Did you know?
Some people can write or draw with both hands at the same time!

So?

Trace and complete this letter pattern.

nonono

Turn your paper clockwise. The base of this arrow icon should line up with the edge of your desk.

87

STAGE 3 WORKSHEET

1. Hold your pen correctly. 2. Keep your wrist straight. 3. Don't hold too tight!

Here is Joe's address.

Copy Joe's address.

Mr Joe Hall

36 Greenfield Avenue

Stratford-upon-Avon

Warwickshire

Now write your own name and address.

Your name

House number and street name

Town or city

County (or State)

Do you know your post code (or Zip Code)?

Turn your paper clockwise. The base of this arrow icon should line up with the edge of your desk.

STAGE 3 WORKSHEET 22

1. Hold your pen correctly. 2. Keep your wrist straight. 3. Don't hold too tight!

Now write your own personal fact file.
Fill in these facts using the words below, or by making up your own.

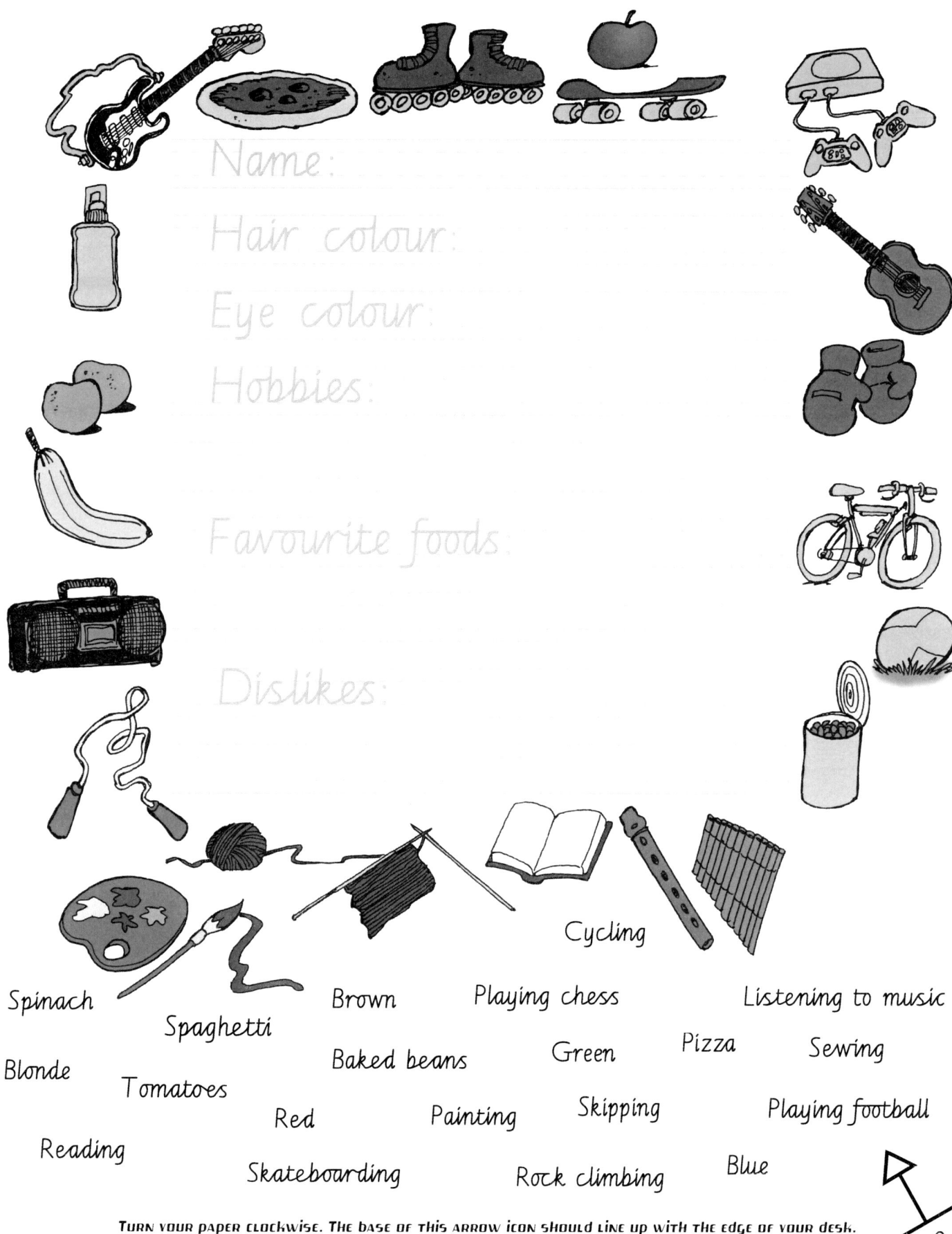

Name:

Hair colour:

Eye colour:

Hobbies:

Favourite foods:

Dislikes:

Cycling

Spinach Brown Playing chess Listening to music
Spaghetti   Green   Pizza   Sewing
Blonde   Baked beans
Tomatoes
Red Painting Skipping Playing football
Reading
Skateboarding Rock climbing Blue

Turn your paper clockwise. The base of this arrow icon should line up with the edge of your desk.

89

STAGE 3 WORKSHEET 23

1. Hold your pen correctly. 2. Keep your wrist straight. 3. Don't hold too tight!

Pencils have been around since the 16th Century.

Copy the pencil-making instructions.

Mix graphite powder with clay.

Roll into a long thin bar. Fire in a kiln.

Dip into wax. Put the thin bar into a

groove cut into a piece of wood and

glue another piece of wood on top.

Did you know?
The first pencils were made from graphite found in Cumbria in Northern England. The graphite was used for marking sheep.

Turn your paper clockwise. The base of this arrow icon should line up with the edge of your desk.

90

STAGE 3 WORKSHEET 24

1. Hold your pen correctly. 2. Keep your wrist straight. 3. Don't hold too tight!

Victorian children had to practise their writing in 'copybooks'.

They learnt to write in a 'copperplate' handwriting style.
They copied out a sentence many times, usually a proverb or a piece of useful information.
They were very careful not to 'blot their copybook'.

Copy these proverbs.

Birds of a feather flock together.

Great oaks from little acorns grow.

Time and tide wait for no man.

Two heads are better than one.

Did you know?
Until the 1970's, school desks each had a small inkwell in them for pupils to dip their pens into.

Turn your paper clockwise. The base of this arrow icon should line up with the edge of your desk.

1. Hold your pen correctly. 2. Keep your wrist straight. 3. Don't hold too tight!

STAGE 3 WORKSHEET 25

The Minoans were Bronze Age people

living on the island of Crete. They led a very civilised life. They had a written language which we call 'Linear A'. Archaeologists have still not managed to decipher it. 'Linear A' gradually changed into a new written language called 'Linear B'. This was deciphered in 1952 by a British architect, Michael Ventris.

Copy this information.

Samuel Morse developed a method of sending a code of dots and dashes by electric telegraph.

It was used at sea until 1993.

Did you know? A cipher is a secret code or the key to a code. Morse Code is a cipher. It was invented by an American, Samuel Morse, in 1844.

Did you know? SOS is a distress call used at sea and comes from the Morse Code signal.

Turn your paper clockwise. The base of this arrow icon should line up with the edge of your desk.

STAGE 3 WORKSHEET 26

1. Hold your pen correctly.   2. Keep your wrist straight.   3. Don't hold too tight!

During World War Two, the Germans invented a machine called Enigma to make coded messages which they thought would never be deciphered. Polish and British mathematicians eventually cracked this code.

Copy these messages.

Meet in the cafe at ten past two.

Look out for a man with a dog.

Pass this message to the guard.

Use the alphabet on the side of the page to crack this message.

Did you know?
Spies often used invisible ink for their messages. You can make your own with lemon juice. When the message has faded it can be revealed by careful ironing.

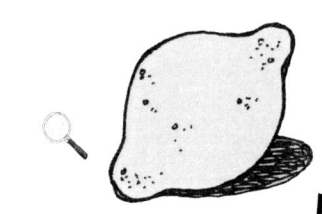

Turn your paper clockwise. The base of this arrow icon should line up with the edge of your desk.

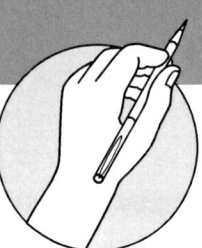

1. Hold your pen correctly. 2. Keep your wrist straight. 3. Don't hold too tight!

STAGE 3 WORKSHEET

Handwriting is one of the most important inventions ever.

Most of what we know about the past comes from written records. Even in this electronic age, handwriting is a useful skill. A person's handwriting is unique. Some official documents are still handwritten.

Did you know? A man called Samuel Pepys kept a diary from 1660 to 1669. He described the Fire of London and the Great Plague amongst other things. He wrote his diary in code. It was deciphered in 1825.

Copy Samuel Pepys' diary entry.

3rd September 1666

I woke in the night to the sound of people running and shouting.

There was a terrible smell of smoke.

Samuel Pepys

Turn your paper clockwise. The base of this arrow icon should line up with the edge of your desk.

STAGES 2 AND 3
REFERENCE SHEET

1 2 3 4 5

6 7 8 9 0

Use this page as a handy reference.

Remember to hold your pencil correctly.

PRACTICE SHEET

You can photocopy this page and use it for more practice.

Remember to line up the base of this icon with the edge of your table.

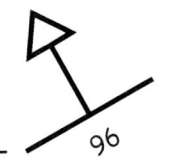

more help for left-handers

Many products have been designed for use with the left hand. There are also specialist centres which offer advice for left-handers, their parents and teachers, and which supply products for left-handed use. Some of the items which relate to activities in this book are described below, but there are many other invaluable everyday devices available for both children and adults. These range from sloping desks to can openers, scissors to secateurs and even golf clubs and electric guitars. A few of the centres around the world which supply products for left-handers, or offer educational advice on left-handed issues, are listed below.

The authors of the *Left Hand Writing Skills* series have also produced a video, *Left-Handed Children – A Guide for Teachers and Parents.* Endorsed by the UK Teacher Training Agency, this is in extensive use throughout Teacher Training Colleges. The video, and many other useful items, may be obtained through the authors' own website – *leftshoponline.co.uk* – or by post from Left 'n' Write Ltd, at the address on the next page.

Educational Products

Pens, Pencils and Sharpeners

Faber Castell's Jumbo triangular pencils, with raised resin dots for extra purchase for the fingers, are excellent. Available separately or in packs of 6 or 12 crayons, Jumbos are a good size for young children. There is also a thinner version called Grip 2001 which has raised resin dots.

YORO refillable pencils and colouring pencils have a rubber adjustable tripod grip and have been specifically designed to make space between the writing and the fingers. Shorter, child-size YORO pencils are also available.

Stabilo produce an excellent pen called the 'Smove Easy'. It is ergonomically designed and has space for both the thumb and forefinger moulded into the barrel. Although a roller ball, it is actually a cartridge pen. Each time a new cartridge is inserted, a new nib is automatically introduced. The ink is erasable.

Stabilo's Trio Max felt tip pens have a triangular grip zone which encourage correct grip – vital for left-handers. They are erasable, use washable ink and are non-toxic.

There are also left-handed pencil sharpeners. These are held in the right hand, and the pencil is turned away from the body. Usually with two holes, the larger hole offers reasonable sharpening for triangular pencils.

Scissors

These can be either right- or left-handed, *not* both. Proper left-handed scissors have the blades set so that, when held either way up in the left hand, the cutting edge is clearly visible on the inside of the scissors. Not being able to use scissors, particularly at a young age, can cause frustration and loss of self-esteem.

Further Reading

The Left-hander's Handbook by Diane G Paul
Published by Robinswood Press.
ISBN 978-1-869981-594

Left Hand Writing Skills

Mark and Heather Stewart

© Mark and Heather Stewart, 2005 and 2006.
Mark Stewart and Heather Stewart have asserted their rights under the Copyright, Designs and Patents Act 1988 to be identified as the authors of this work.

Design and layout by Lorraine Payne.
Illustrations © Fred Chevalier, 2005 and 2006.
Worksheets set in Sassoon Infant and GDI Combined (modified).
Printed by Blueprint Design & Graphics Ltd, Stourbridge.

All rights reserved. No part of this publication may be reproduced, stored in a retrieval system or transmitted in any form, or by any means, electronic, mechanical, photocopying, recording or otherwise, without prior permission in writing from the publisher.

The publisher, however, hereby authorises individual specialist literacy and other teachers to take, without the prior permission in writing of the publisher, photocopies of any pages from this book for use exclusively in teaching and homework situations within the limits of one teaching establishment only.

Robinswood Press South Avenue Stourbridge DY8 3XY

Robinswood
robinswoodpress.com

Stourbridge England   Calgary Canada
Dublin Republic of Ireland

ISBN 978-1-869981-839

Useful Contacts for left-handers

Left 'n' Write Ltd
5 Charles Street Worcester WR1 2AQ
leftshoponline.co.uk
P +44 (0)1905 25798

Wise Owl Toys
Worcester
P +44 (0)1905 222353
Dorchester
P +44 (0)1305 266311
wiseowltoys.co.uk

STA Ltd
252 Harolds Cross Road
Dublin 6W Ireland
staeducational.com
P +353 (0)1 4966688

Lefty's – Left Handed Products and Resource Centre
PO Box 6033 Blacktown BC
New South Wales 2148 Australia
leftys.com.au
P +61 (0)2 9676 7215

The National Handwriting Association
nha-handwriting.org.uk

Anything Left-Handed Ltd
Sterling House 18 Avenue Road Belmont
Surrey SM2 6JD
anythingleft-handed.co.uk
P +44 (0)20 8770 3722